BOOK ANALYSIS

Written by Jeremy Lambert
Translated by Rebecca Neal

Secondhand Time

BY SVETLANA ALEXIEVICH

SVETLANA ALEXIEVICH

BELORUSSIAN JOURNALIST AND PROSE WRITER

- **Born in Stanislav, Ukraine, USSR (now Ivano-Frankivsk, Ukraine) in 1948.**
- **Notable works:**
  - *The Unwomanly Face of War* (1985), collection of testimonies
  - *Boys in Zinc* (1991), collection of testimonies
  - *Chernobyl Prayer: A Chronicle of the Future* (1999), collection of testimonies

Svetlana Alexievich was born in Ukraine shortly after the end of the Second World War (1939-1945), but moved to Belarus with her family at a young age. She studied journalism in Minsk, graduating in 1972, and went on to work for a number of Belorussian newspapers and magazines throughout the 1970s and 1980s. In 1983, she joined the Union of Soviet Writers.

Her books, which were all originally written in Russian, interweave a multitude of eyewitness accounts of major events and historical periods, are closely linked to the Communist society she lived in, and often feature scathing criticism of Ukrainian, Belorussian and Russian policies, which meant that they were initially censored. After living abroad for over a decade, she moved back to Minsk in 2011.

She was awarded the Nobel Prize in Literature in 2015.

SECONDHAND TIME

A MOSAIC OF ACCOUNTS OF A LOST EMPIRE

- **Genre:** collection of testimonies
- **Reference edition:** Alexievich, S. (2016) *Secondhand Time: The Last of the Soviets*. Trans. Shayevich, B. New York: Random House.
- **1st edition:** 2013
- **Themes:** Soviet Union, Communism, political transition, capitalism, Russian history

In *Secondhand Time*, Svetlana Alexievich compiles a series of accounts to create a varied, complex, detailed picture of the political transformation that Russian society underwent in the two decades following the dissolution of the USSR in 1991. This period of profound change encompassed major economic shifts, civil wars in the peripheral republics of the former nation and a growing sense of being culturally adrift. The book's strength lies in the fact that the author does not address these issues directly, but rather explores them through personal accounts from everyday people which focus on their own stories, memories, family histories and love affairs.

SUMMARY

A TWO-PART STRUCTURE

Secondhand Time is a collection of testimonies focusing on the period immediately following the establishment of the Russian Federation in 1991. The country's exceptionally socially, ethnically and culturally diverse population had previously lived under a decades-long totalitarian regime which used unifying myths (political power, an invincible army, the space race, etc.) and symbols of inclusion (Communist youth organisations, commitment to the party, colonisation, etc.) in an attempt to impose a uniform view of reality on the entire country. When this regime collapsed, its citizens were faced with an entirely new and unfamiliar political, economic and social system.

The participants' accounts span two decades, from 1991 to 2012, and are divided into two parts:

- The first part, **"The Consolation of Apocalypse"**, is made up of accounts gathered between 1991 and 2001, when Boris Yeltsin (Russian politician, 1931-2007) was president of the Russian Federation. This period saw the development of unfettered capitalism in the countries of the former USSR, which facilitated the rise of a new class of oligarchs who became billionaires by monopolising large swathes of the national economy, often through dubious methods. The total area of the Russian Federation also shrank during this period, as a number of the former states of the USSR began clamouring for independence. These included Armenia, Azerbaijan, Georgia, Chechnya (which still forms part of the Russian Federation, although it enjoys a degree of political independence), Estonia, Latvia, Lithuania, Ukraine and Belarus. The views of the individuals spoken to in this part vary depend on their social status and nationality.

- The second part, **"The Charms of Emptiness"**, focuses on the period from 2002 to 2012, which was marked by the increasing concentration of power in the hands of Vladimir Putin (Russian politician, born in 1952), the struggle against the oligarchs, the wars in Chechnya, the independence of the peripheral republics and the increasing impoverishment of ordinary citizens, who no longer received support from the government to purchase basic products. The accounts in this section all address these issues differently, and have a more nostalgic tone than those in the first part.

Each of these two parts comprises ten "stories", the titles of which all take the form "On..." (for example, "On the Sweetness of Suffering and the Trick of the Russian Soul" and "On Courage and What Comes After"). Both parts are preceded by fragments grouped together under the title "Snatches of Street Noise and Kitchen Conversations". These fragments are anonymous statements which are presented without context, so all we know is the decade they date from. Taken as a whole, they give a comprehensive, multi-dimensional view of the socio-political setting of the following ten stories. The book also features a chronology of Russian history after Stalin's death and an introductory section entitled "Remarks from an Accomplice", which outlines the author's point of view.

We are not told much about how Alexievich gathered her accounts: all we learn is that they are excerpts from conversations that were recorded or transcribed. Brief comments from the author, which are written in italics and are reminiscent of stage directions, indicate that she met the participants in a range of locations, in provinces and cities within Russia and even abroad. The people she has spoken to come from very different social and professional backgrounds, from secretaries of the regional Party committees to former fighters to immigrant workers. Their "stories" all take the form of a monologue, meaning that the author's questions are not recorded.

A MOSAIC OF VIEWPOINTS

Together, these different voices form a mosaic which gives a nuanced insight into a society grappling with one of the major political phenomena of the 20th century, namely socialism. The diversity of viewpoints results in a comprehensive depiction of post-Soviet society, which is made up of both people who have succumbed to disillusionment and a smaller number of individuals who have managed to prosper in this new situation. Personal disappointments often mingle with reflections on the nature of the state, on the things that were better before, and on the things that have got worse in the post-Soviet society, as well as general observations about life. Overall, few of the "stories" take an optimistic view of the change following the collapse of the Soviet Union. These are some positive elements, but they are virtually drowned out by the rhetoric of omnipresent suffering.

It can therefore be said that the central theme of the book is suffering. The various participants make reference to:

- the imprisonment, deportment and death of loved ones under Stalin's regime (1929-1953);
- personal heartache;
- differences in mindsets (in particular between a parent who grew up during the Soviet era and a child who grew up after the collapse of the USSR);
- problems linked to ethnic origin;
- social problems such as alcoholism and extreme poverty.

These fragmentary biographies feature recurring elements which help to build up a picture of Soviet society as a whole, the period of political transition and the resulting liberal system. Each participant contributes to this picture by adding fragments of their daily life, their view of events and their feelings and emotions. The fact that their opinions differ mean that the overall picture is full of contradictions; it is also incomplete, as the author has chosen what to include and what to leave out. However, the book's form, the harmony of the work as a whole and the subjects it has chosen to address make it an immensely powerful depiction of a turbulent historical period.

CONTEXT

THE HISTORY OF THE USSR

The Union of Soviet Socialist Republics (USSR) emerged in the wake of the October Revolution in 1917. The new state, which officially came into existence on 30 December 1922, took the form of a federation of republics which were each relatively autonomous. The Communist Party, which purportedly represented the proletariat, the victor of the class struggle, directed economic, social, military and cultural activity within the nation through the Politburo. This control was enforced by the People's Commissariat for Internal Affairs, better known under its acronym NKVD, which functioned as a political police force. The first leader of the USSR was Vladimir Lenin (1870-1924); in the power struggle that followed his death, Joseph Stalin (1878-1953) outmanoeuvred his main rival Leon Trotsky (1879-1940) to assume leadership of the country.

Stalin initially positioned himself as Lenin's natural political successor, then as the only person who could truly interpret and implement his ideas. He methodically eliminated any suspected political opponents, both within the Party and in wider society. Under his dictatorial regime, terror, which had been present in the USSR since its inception, became more intense and widespread.

Although the USSR initially allied itself with Germany in the Second World War, Hitler's troops attacked the country in June 1941. The Battle of Stalingrad (July 1942-February 1943), one of the deadliest confrontations in history, ended in victory for the Soviets, enabling them to launch a counter-offensive which soon saw them reach the outskirts of Berlin. After playing a crucial role in the Allied fight against fascism, Stalin was able to impose a stranglehold over much of Central and Eastern Europe.

Stalin died in 1953 and was succeeded by Nikita Khrushchev (1894-1971). At the 20th Congress of the Communist Party of the Soviet Union in 1956, Khrushchev delivered a speech in which he openly criticised the cult of personality instigated by his predecessor. This was a key moment in the so-called Thaw, when censorship and repression within the USSR were relaxed somewhat. At the same time, the Cold War (1945-1990) between the USA and USSR was worsening and tensions between the two countries were running increasingly high.

Khrushchev was removed from power in 1964 and replaced by Leonid Brezhnev (1906-1982), whose two decades at the head of the country were characterised by economic and cultural stagnation. In spite of this lack of progress, Brezhnev espoused the theory that the USSR had become the model of true socialism, which justified everything that had led up to this point – including Stalinism. In 1979, the USSR went to war in Afghanistan, with terrible consequences for Soviet troops.

After a series of short-lived leaders in the early 1980s, Mikhail Gorbachev (born in 1931) became General Secretary of the Communist Party of the Soviet Union. He embarked on a programme of reform known as *perestroika* ("restructuring"), with measures including the introduction of private-sector activity on a small scale, tolerance of some political pluralism (although he held fast to the belief that the Communist Party should run the country) and the signature of treaties with the USA.

THE TRANSITION TO DEMOCRACY

After the fall of the Berlin Wall in 1989 and the collapse of Communist regimes across Central and Eastern Europe, the USSR tried to hold onto its position through a programme of systemic reform. However, in August 1991, when Gorbachev was on holiday in Crimea, a group of hardline Party members seized the opportunity to launch a coup, which was thwarted thanks to opposition from ordinary people and the army. Gorbachev was still the country's leader, but was unable to prevent the dissolution of the Communist Party, which marked the end of the USSR.

Yeltsin was then elected president of the newly-created Russian Federation. A number of republics claimed their independence, including Armenia, Azerbaijan and Georgia, all of which then played host to territorial conflicts. The First Chechen War, which was fought over the oil-rich region of Chechnya, broke out in 1994, and although a provisional peace treaty was signed in May 1997, hostilities resumed in 1999. The 1990s also saw skyrocketing inflation in the former Soviet Republics. Many businesses were swiftly privatised, and unemployment, which was previously unheard of in the country, became widespread. Companies were so short of ready money that they were forced to pay their employees in manufactured products, and oligarchs seized large swathes of the Russian economy for their own personal gain.

As a result of these circumstances, Yeltsin's popularity plummeted, and in December 1999 he resigned. He was replaced by Vladimir Putin, who served two terms as president and then became prime minister before returning to the presidency in 2012. Under his leadership, political opposition has been harshly repressed and close surveillance has become widespread. Oligarchs who oppose his regime have often lost their positions, allowing the state to recover its monopoly over certain sections of the economy. In parallel to this, the Second Chechen War, which only ended in 2009, and the terrorist attacks which accompanied it have led to widespread trauma within Russian society.

ANALYSIS

ALEXIEVICH'S APPROACH

Alexievich outlines her approach in the opening pages of her book: "I'm trying to honestly hear out all the participants of the old socialist drama..." (p. 3). She makes no attempt to hide her contempt for the repressive political system she grew up under and actively participated in (she was a member of socialist youth movements, and later of the Union of Soviet Writers). It is therefore unsurprising that when she evokes the *"Homo sovieticus"*, a new kind of man created by the Soviet system, she then says "I am this person" (*ibid*.). This idea subsequently recurs in the short comments in italics that accompany the accounts: "At first, I didn't believe my ears when I heard someone singing 'Moscow Nights', our favourite Soviet song. When I go back into the room, everyone is singing along. I am, too" (p. 388). She never positions herself as an outsider or a stranger to the world she is describing:

"People who've come out of socialism are both like and unlike the rest of humanity – we have our own lexicon, our own conceptions of good and evil, our heroes, our martyrs. We have a special relationship with death." (p. 3)

While she carefully records the accounts of her participants, Alexievich's approach is shaped by her sensibilities as a writer: "I look at the world as a writer and not a historian. I am fascinated by people" (p. 7). That said, she admits that she is producing a work of memory, which makes her work similar to that of a historian, but "a cold-blooded historian, not one who is holding a blazing torch" (p. 74). By this, she means that she is not shaping her text to fit a preconceived idea.

She is interested in details from everyday life, which for her are what make up the *Homo sovieticus*. When she conducts her interviews, "I don't ask people about socialism, I want to know about love, jealousy, childhood, old age. Music, dances, hairdos. The myriad sundry details of a vanished way of life" (p. 7). However, the one subject that predominates throughout all the accounts is suffering, which is repeatedly evoked by the participants and by the author herself in her comments.

HOMO SOVIETICUS AND RELATIVISM

Alexievich opens her book by expressing her desire to explore the various facets of the *Homo sovieticus*. This term, which is used to refer to Soviet citizens and has largely negative connotations, was popularised by the Russian writer Aleksandr Zinoviev (1922-2006), who wrote a book of the same name. These individuals are characterised by a willingness to settle for less, a lack of interest in both their work and its results, the rejection of any personal responsibility and the passive acceptance of orders from above. Alexievich stresses these traits in the opening section of her book: "Communism had an insane plan: to remake the 'old breed of man,' ancient Adam. And it really worked... perhaps it was communism's only achievement" (p. 3). For the author, the *Homo sovieticus* is the only truly new thing to come out of Soviet society.

She is quick to highlight the paradoxical nature of this situation: "People didn't recognize their own slavery – they even liked being slaves" (p. 4). This paradox leads to a particular outlook on the world, which is grounded in widespread suffering but rejects the materialism of the West. The *Homo sovieticus* has nothing, but is surrounded by people who also have nothing. Most importantly, this shared suffering makes everybody equal: they all live in the same bleak, mundane environment with little idea of what is happening in the outside world, which seems distant because of the vastness of their own country.

When the country embarked on its transition to capitalism, most people did not hope for radical change, but rather for development, modification or evolution. This can be seen in *perestroika*, Gorbachev's programme of gradual reform. One anonymous participant tells the author: "Most people were not anti-Soviet; they only wanted to live well" (p. 20). Alexievich seems to agree with this assessment: she had previously explained that few people actually wanted a change of regime, and that many of them even seemed irritated by the idea of liberty. This intermediate position, with the people seeming to hesitate between hope for development and a desire for more of the same, resulted in a kind of destructive relativism based on the people's passive acceptance of their appalling living conditions and the idea that there was no other way. The passage below is a striking example of this attitude:

> "Uncle Vanya [...] came back [from the camps] with a withered hand, toothless, his liver enlarged. He went back to work at the same factory, at the same job, in the same office, same desk. [...] He sat across from the guy who'd informed on him. Everyone knew it and Uncle Vann knew it, too [...] And so on that's us! Our life! That's what we're like!" (pp. 272-273).

Another participant expresses this relativism in the form of an aphorism: "Human truth is just a nail that everybody hangs their hats on" (p. 122).

This constant tension between resistance and disaffection shapes the stories told in *Secondhand Time*, and helps to illustrate the complexity of the changes that were taking place within Soviet society.

A CHANGING SOCIETY

The participants in the book compare their current lives to their lives under Communism, in particular by referring to material possessions and everyday objects. This leads to the emergence of a dichotomy that runs throughout the book, contrasting money, which seems to be omnipresent, and a lost ideal:

> "This country is foreign to me. It's foreign! It used to be that when people came over, we'd talk about books, plays... Now it's who bought what? What's the exchange rate?" (p. 266)
> "You have nothing. Just comfort. Anything for a full belly... Those stomachs of yours... Stuff your face and fill your house with tchotchkes. But I... my generation... We built everything you have. The factories, the dams, the electric power stations. What have you ever built? And we were the ones who defeated Hitler." (p. 184)
> "My younger brother would wash cars after class, sell chewing gum and other junk in the subway and he made more money than our father – our father who was a scientist. A PhD! The Soviet elite!" (p. 162)

Conversely, descriptions of the Communist period are characterised by pervasive violence. That said, a number of other elements are described alongside it:

- **The one-dimensional view of the world spread by the authorities**. One participant says: "I buy three newspapers and each one of them has its own version of the truth. Where's the real truth? You used to be able to get up in the morning, read *Pravda*, and know all you needed to know, understand everything you needed to understand" (p. 6).

- **The omnipresence of books and the writings of intellectuals**: "we picked up a mimeographed copy of Nadezhda Mandelstam's memoirs, which everyone was reading at the time" (p. 157).
- **Patriotic songs**. These are scattered throughout the text, and inspire a sense of nostalgia in the participants: "With gentle light, the morning paints/The ancient Kremlin walls./The whole Soviet nation/Awakens with the dawn. It's a pretty song. To me, it's still pretty" (p. 254).
- **Great deeds**, such as victory over fascism in the Great Patriotic War, the space race and Yuri Garagin's (1934-1968) achievement of being the first person to reach outer space, and the development of nuclear power.
- **The kitchens in ordinary citizens' apartments**, which are seen as safe places where thoughts and opinions can be freely expressed: "We lived in our kitchens. The whole country

lived in their kitchens. You'd go to somebody's house, drink wine, listen to songs, talk about poetry. There's an open tin can, slices of black bread. Everyone's happy" (p. 156).

By contrast, the post-Soviet period is symbolised by:

- **The possibility of buying salami, which was previously rationed**: "People dreamt that tons of salami would appear at the stores at Soviet prices and members of the Politburo would stand in line for it along with the rest of us. Salami is a benchmark of our existence" (p. 162).
- **Consumer goods, and the violence that people are prepared to resort to in order to get their hands on them**: "We live in a big building with twenty entrances. Every morning, they'd find another body in the courtyard – eventually, we stopped being shocked. Real capitalism was here" (p. 32).
- **The emergence of economic theories** and terms such as "voucher" and "trader".
- **The resurgence of the Church as part of everyday life**: "Everyone had started going to church, and my grandma did, too. She'd cross

herself and keep the fasts, but the only thing she ever really believed in was communism" (p. 321).

In the accounts that make up the book, the moment of transition stands out for the omnipresence of the media: "He read the papers all day long. In the morning, he'd run down to the Publisher's Union kiosk by our house with a big shopping bag. He listened to the radio and watched TV nonstop. Everyone was a bit nuts at the time" (p. 221).

VIOLENCE

The central theme of the accounts is suffering, which is linked to the violence that permeates them. Throughout its entire existence, the USSR was constantly on a war footing to protect itself against its "enemies", both real and perceived. Violence was at the heart of Soviet life and was always justified by the regime, to such a point that it began to seem normal. It took various forms, including censorship, self-censorship, informing and the fear of being informed on. A vast number of Soviet citizens were sent to labour camps, which sprang up across the country as soon as it was established. Maria Voiteshonok, a 57-year-old writer, describes her life by saying: "Suffering brought me up" (p. 235).

A number of the participants are struck by the lack of condemnations when the Soviet Union collapsed. While one businessman insists that "I consider Stalin as bad as Hitler, I demand Nuremberg trials for those Red bitches" (p. 137), more moderate individuals take an equivocal stance towards everyday violence, which illustrates just how deeply ingrained it was in Soviet society. The passage below illustrates the complexity of the issue:

> "Here's a question: Who made Stalin Stalin? There's the problem of responsibility...
> Should you only put people on trial if they actually murdered and tortured people or:
> should it also be the informants...
> the people who took the children of 'enemies of the people' away from their relatives and sent them to orphanages...
> the drivers who transported the arrested...
> the cleaning women who washed the floors after people were tortured...
> the director of the railways that conveyed political prisoners to the north in cattle cars...

the tailors who sewed camp guards' coats. The doctors who did their dental work, took their cardiograms, all so that they could better withstand the stresses of their jobs…" (p. 360)

Conversely, the violence engendered by conflicts of personal interest after the fall of the USSR inspires widespread hatred and comes to symbolise the period of transition: "the local 'capitalists' [...] walked around surrounded by men with machine guns" (p. 344); "They're pillaging, tearing Russia into little pieces" (p. 416).

NOSTALGIA FOR RUSSIA'S FORMER GLORY

The most sensitive paradox in the book is the nostalgia for Russian greatness before and during the Communist period, in spite of the violence that was used to maintain it during the Soviet era. Numerous participants use the term "empire" to refer to both Tsarist Russia and the USSR: "We had a great empire – stretching from sea to sea, from beyond the Arctic to the subtropics" (p. 166). The corollary to this idea is the need for a strong leader who can secure the country's borders and prove its greatness. One participant, who is a particularly strong supporter of socialism, exclaims: "The people want simple things. A surplus of ginger-snaps. And a Tsar! [...] Our country has a tsarist mentality, it's subconsciously tsarist. Genetically. Everyone needs a Tsar" (p. 125).

It is therefore unsurprising that, even half a century after his death, Stalin still looms large in many of the accounts, although he is arguably a less terrifying figure than during his reign of violent repression. He is seen less as a flesh and blood man, and more as the authority figure who ruled over generations of Soviet citizens. While some participants describe him using empty clichés ("Stalin entered the Russia of the wooden plow and left it with the atom bomb", p. 263), others are more direct: "In short, we reminisce about the Soviet era. Do you understand? Our conversations always end the same way: 'It's a mess out there. We need a Stalin'" (p. 270).

Conversely, Gorbachev, who introduced a new form of socialism and took the first steps towards a market economy and all the distortions and imbalances that accompanied it, is seen as weak, indecisive and overly willing to compromise: one high-ranking socialist bureaucrat criticises his weakness by saying "Gorbachev ceded power without any bloodshed" (p. 125).

When the participants talk about their country today, which is just one nation among many and is less powerful and influential than it once was, their disenchantment shines through. This disenchantment is complex in nature and has numerous causes. Although many Soviet citizens dreamed of freedom of expression when they lived under the Soviet regime, the hunger and shortages that have arisen under the new capitalist system often leave them yearning for the Communist past.

FURTHER REFLECTION

SOME QUESTIONS TO THINK ABOUT...

- What are the limitations of the objectivity that Alexievich strives towards in *Secondhand Time*?
- Alexievich presents herself as a pure product of Soviet society. Which elements of her life story support this idea?
- Can Alexievich be considered a Belorussian author, even though she was born in Ukraine and writes in Russian?
- How is the "Russian soul" described in *Secondhand Time*?
- Ivano-Frankivsk, the city where Alexievich was born, has belonged to numerous countries and been governed by various political regimes since the start of the 20th century. List these countries and regimes. Do you think that this aspect of its history has influenced its inhabitants, and the author in particular?

- To what extent has Stalin's role in the history of the USSR been condemned and then rehabilitated by Soviet historians? How is he viewed now?
- What do you think of the form the author has chosen to explore the subjects tackled in her book?
- Is the vision of Communism set out in *Secondhand Time* consistent with the way it is viewed in the West? What, if anything, surprised you in the accounts featured in the book?
- How did the Nobel Prize Committee describe Alexievich's work in 2015? Comment on this description.

We want to hear from you!
Leave a comment on your online library
and share your favourite books on social media!

FURTHER READING

REFERENCE EDITION

- Alexievich, S. (2016) *Secondhand Time: The Last of the Soviets*. Trans. Shayevich, B. New York: Random House.

www.brightsummaries.com

Ebook EAN: 9782808009720

Paperback EAN: 9782808009737

Legal Deposit: D/2018/12603/242

Cover: © Primento

Digital conception by Primento, the digital partner of
publishers.

Made in the USA
Middletown, DE
11 July 2022